DON'T MOVE MY GOAL POST!

A Fearless Teen Boy's Guide to Career Planning and Future Success

Dare to Dream Big and Be the Coach of Your Life

Ariana Smith

ISBN 978-9916-9870-2-5 (eBook)
ISBN 978-9916-9870-1-8 (paperback)
ISBN 978-9916-9870-0-1 (hardcover)

www.ariana-smith.com

What's Inside

Ticket to All Games—No Limit to Your Choices!

Something for You!

Get your printable templates today!

At the end of each chapter, you will find cool personal tasks, which can be completed in your notebook. You can also get print-ready templates (including templates for daily tasks, weekly goals, project lists, and a distraction list) for free!

Scan this code to download.

Prologue

Congratulations! You opened the book! After all, how bad can a book be that has the words 'goal post' in its title, right? This book IS going to be about goals, not necessarily like the one at the end of a soccer or football field. Relax, you aren't going to have to make any big decisions! You are just going to find out what's important for you to do right now in your life, and what's not so important. This means you can sit back, grab some munchies, and read! Chill!

Imagine yourself in a great big hot air balloon. It's one of those striped balloons—this one has alternate blue and red stripes on the sides. You can hear the propane jet squishing noise, almost like the sound of a train passing by. The fire blast is what keeps the balloon full above your head. As you hold onto the edges of the basket, maybe you are a little afraid of going so far up in the sky, but you are excited, too! Hot air rises, and so, with a great big swooshing sound, the blue and red balloon lifts you up, up, up into the air. Higher and higher you go!

You begin to see everything below you. You are higher than the trees, as your blue and yellow balloon silently floats along. Below you, you see the football field, and you can see both goal posts! You can see birds flying right near you. Your hands might even loosen their grip on the basket you are flying in, just a bit. You take a big breath. This feels great! You feel so great that you want to go soaring into blue skies again and again.

Like all adventures in your life, soaring in a hot air balloon takes practice. You need instructions on how to "drive the balloon." You can't just get into the balloon and take off toward the clouds. For example, even if you can take off, *how do you get back down?* Yes, you must first learn how to take off and land in a hot air balloon.

All learning happens from experiences you have, or from reading information, or from studying, or sometimes, another person teaches you what they know. Learning is a part of every successful life. In fact, we humans start learning from the moment we are born until the day we leave this world.

Once you are soaring in your life, just as if you are in a hot air balloon, you can look down and see things you did not see previously.

In the hot air balloon, you can see the whole town below you, and people look so small. You are higher than the trees, or even the tallest buildings in the distance. You have an excellent view of everything.

In your life, experience and learning can help you have a better view of your world.

This is how this book hopes to be for you. Hopefully, you will soar above everything currently going on in your life, for you to get a nice bird's eye view of what your future world and life can be. Ideally, you will get a leg-up on what's important in your life right now, and what you must learn or what steps you must take, to help you along your life's ride, and what things you can just coast and not worry or fret over.

Keep soaring and enjoy your ride!

Chapter One

What Game Are You Playing?

Some people believe life is like a game. That's an interesting concept, especially when you consider the video games you might be playing every day. *Do you play video games? Do some of the video games you play seem like real life?* Some video games have graphics so real, they do appear like real life.[1] You know they aren't real, but they are fun to play because they seem so real.

Video games like Kerbal©, where kids can build rockets that work to explore space and the solar system, were actually focused on by NASA because they were so authentic. On Kerbal, you can build an aerodynamic rocket based on orbital physics, and even if you don't have a clue what that is right now, by the time you played Kerbal, you would know a lot about what that means! Playing Kerbal would instruct you.

How *is playing video games like your own life?* You are a creative individual, aren't you? When you play a video game you must creatively solve problems. You must be in control of your own "life" (or your own joystick), but in a video game like Minecraft©, you must also not only be self-directed, and self-aware, but you must also collaborate with other people to reach a certain goal or objective. This is the same in your "real" life, where you have to get along with your friends and classmates and work together. This teamwork is often essential for you to win in the video game—and likewise, teamwork is important in the "real" game of life. Along the way, you must also utilize skills you have learned in life, actually in your 'real' life—skills such as reading and mathematics.

Many parents feel that video game playing is disruptive to their children because it's so much like real life. Parents, as a general rule, allow their children to play 2.2 hours per day of video games.[2] *How many hours do you play video games? Are the games you play like your real life or are they just imaginary games?*

Real life is often described using phrases like 'the game of life,' or 'walk of life,' or even 'the river of life,' or 'life's road,' or 'life's journey.' *What do you think is the most important thing to acquire in the real 'game of life'?* If you said, "getting an education," you are correct. One of the most important things for a boy your age to realize is that you must learn how to read, and how to do basic math, at the very least. This means you must plan to graduate from high school. What you choose to do after that might range from starting your own business, going to a special trade school, joining the military, or going to college, or maybe traveling the world. If you make sure you have a good, solid, basic education first, you will be able to pick and choose which direction you want to travel in next.

Believe it or not, sadly, there ARE students who graduate from high school without knowing how to read or how to compute basic math. Somehow, these students just kind of float through school, but the gaps in their education quickly pile up. More on 'gaps' later . . .

Has a grandparent ever squeezed your cheeks and asked you, "What do you want to be when you grow up?" If not your grandparent, then someone else in your life might have asked you that question. These well-meaning people may stare down at you with a very solemn look on their faces when they ask the question. *Do you have an answer? Must you have an answer? Is it important for you to know right this moment what you want to "be" when you grow up?* You might just find some of the answers to those questions in this book.

Defining Your Dream

First, the good news: no, you don't have to tell the world right this moment *what you want to be when you grow up.* Perhaps you aren't even quite sure yet what your interests truly are. Yet, here's the truth—you are IN the game of life, like it or not, and in this game of real life, eventually, most people decide what their dreams are, and they take steps to achieve them. Everyone likes a dream-come-true, right? Well, first, you have to know, *kind of,* what that dream of yours might be.

Do you know that over 80% of the adults living today had a dream when they were a child? Yep, these adults had a dream, but they let go of their dream. 58% of these adults wish they had never let go of their dream.[3] *Why do you think someone would let go of a dream?* The main reason a child must let go of a dream is because they did not prepare for their dream come true in the first place. There are often steps that must be taken prior to achieving success with one's dream. Sometimes, these planning steps may have to begin very early in life. Most kids don't know that. It just depends on what your dream is.

But here's the good news! You are still a kid. Wow! *What does that mean?* It means because you are reading this book, you have the opportunity to prepare for your dream, and you have plenty of time to get any knowledge you might need along the way. You will have more tools in your *life skills toolbox* to help you find out what you must do to achieve your goals to reach your dreams. Here are some tools that MUST be in your life skills toolbox, no matter which dream you pursue:

- Reading skills
- Math skills
- Life Management skills
- Organizational skills

Perhaps that small list seems a bit overwhelming right now to you. You do need all those skills, but as you progress along in school, you will naturally develop most of them. You also have the option of adding to your life skills toolbox on your own. You can also fill in the gaps in your education, in fact, a word to the wise: you need to fill in those gaps for you to move towards your dreams. Later in the book, you will get help in defining what your gaps may be.

Important Questions

Let's take a moment so you can begin asking yourself some questions which might help you define some of the things you like to do—some of the things you are good at, or even great at doing, or perhaps, some things that might be giving you trouble in your academic life.

- *Do you like to think about things for a long while before you start to do them?* These questions are important to think about. Sometimes, when you think about things for a long while when you are in school, it can become a problem. *Why?* Because while you are still thinking about things you don't quite "get," the teacher may have already moved on to other parts of the lesson. Now, you might not understand what they just taught, and you might not be tuned in to what the teacher has started to teach next. This is how your education gaps can begin to happen.

- *Would you rather watch a 'how to' video, or try to do something with your hands to figure it out?* If you know you need to have a 'hands-on' approach to learning, as the coach of your own life, it's important that you explain this to your teacher. If your teachers don't believe it's important, go to your counselor. Learn to have a voice for yourself. Remember, no one loves you or cares about you more than you should be caring and loving yourself and taking care of your own needs.

- *Do you like to doodle when your teacher is speaking?* Doodling while your teacher is teaching is NOT a bad thing, as long as you are listening. In fact, doodling might be helping you to stay focused while the teacher is teaching.

- *Do you start umpteen tasks, and then get none of them done by the end of the day?* As far as getting tasks accomplished, prioritizing a "to-do" list each day is an important way to become successful at getting things accomplished. Always put the most important items which need to be attended to each day at the top of your list. Check your list often, marking off what you have accomplished.

- *Are there subjects in school you just don't "get"?* Get help! If you just sit quietly at your desk, or if you act out in class, or skip the class altogether, you won't be able to fill in the knowledge gaps. The gaps will only get wider and wider in what you don't know. Remember, everything you learn in school builds on what you have previously learned. Don't let the 'gaps' turn into sinkholes!

It isn't uncommon for boys to say, "I have so many things I want to do with my life, I don't know WHAT I should concentrate on." You don't have to decide right this moment what you are going to do with the rest of your life, but you do have an obligation to yourself to begin to know where your interests and skills lie. In order for you to ensure you give yourself the best chance to be happy and successful in your life, the time to begin *thinking* about what you like is right this moment!

Some adults study what people want to be when they grow up. They also study if adults who achieve their dreams are happy when they are living their dream. *Do you think people who are living their dreams are happier than people who gave up their dreams?* The answer is, generally, yes, they are happier.

Boys your age mostly say there are ten careers they would like to have when they are an adult. The careers are ranked according to boys' favorites: Professional athlete, doctor, musician, police officer, business owner, superhero, teacher, pharmacist, movie star, architect, firefighter.[4] This list seems limited because it doesn't list jobs such as plumbers, carpenters, air conditioner repairmen, mechanics, linemen, electricians, truck drivers, pilots, sanitary engineers, forest rangers, carpenters, linguists, and many more. However, the top ten jobs are more familiar to boys your age.

The number one job boys your age want to be is a professional athlete. By 2023, there will be only 800 new openings for professional athletes. Professional athlete is a highly competitive field of jobs. Ten years of working in the field of sports is one of the requirements of this career before you even get out the door. The average salary is $58,818.[5] That number might come as a shock to you because most people believe athletes get much more money than that—like, in the millions. Of course, established athletes may also secure some contracts for advertising products, which is what brings in more money for them.[6] *If becoming an athlete is a career choice for you, what can you do to prepare for this career choice? What do you need to do?* Going down 'rabbit holes' on a search on the Internet can bring you lots of information about all of these jobs. It's well worth your time to investigate. Remember, you make yourself a priority when you take the time to do the steps necessary to help yourself succeed!

The second profession boys your age list as a favorite is becoming a doctor. *Do these two occupations have anything in common?* At first thought, that's probably a hard no, but they actually do. Both of these jobs require that you finish high school, not to mention what comes next. You must know how to read and how to do math. 80% of professional athletes have a bachelor's degree, and of course, doctors have degrees all the way up to a PhD—which is what allows them to have the word "doctor" as part of their name.

Life's Patterns

Do you see a pattern here? Some careers have things you must learn BEFORE you graduate high school.

Therefore, it's a little bit important to have a few dreams at this point, so you know what to concentrate on. But the main thing, which is very important, is that you get your reading and math grades up to par. More on how to do this later, too . . .

Number three on the boys' favorite careers list is becoming a musician. That's great! A musician really needs to generally start learning to play an instrument by fourth grade. Yes, you will have to learn to read notes, base clef, and treble clef, and who knows what great heights you will achieve? You might even begin to write your own music. Early prep time for a musician is VERY important. Though you *can* learn how to play an instrument at thirty-years-old, if you want to be a *professional musician*, it's best if you learn to play an instrument at a much younger age. Yes, this means taking music lessons starting at about ten-years-old or younger.

You can see there is somewhat of a pattern here, as well. Some careers in life take early preparation, like way early, in grammar school. Boys generally don't think about that, but you are here reading this book to learn early on in your life that, though you are young, you still have important things to think about and consider.

As *the coach of your own life*, thinking about what early preparation you might need is extremely important. In the old days, learning about careers early on in life wasn't as important. Most boys just became what their fathers were. If their dad was a baker, they became a baker, too. If their dad was a mechanic, they became a mechanic. If their dad was a farmer, they learned to be a farmer. It's just the way it was in the *old days*. Boys generally followed in their father's career footsteps, but this isn't how it is today.

Today, you have many, many choices in your future, though competition can be very strong for certain careers. You can also choose careers which didn't even EXIST in the *old days*.

Helmet & Knee Pad Time

After every chapter in this book, you will see this heading: *Helmet & Knee Pad Time. What is it?* This point in the book is the spot where you, basically, must pause to do a little work and a little planning. When you put on a helmet to play a game, it generally means there is hard work ahead, and maybe a few tumbles. Knee pads mean you might have to get down and do some difficult work, which requires you to prepare. Football players put on helmets and knee pads for protection while they play the game, but here, the heading is a metaphor. A metaphor is just a figure of speech, a word or phrase that uses one thing to describe something else. You aren't actually going to put on a helmet and knee pads to play football—but you are going to prepare for ten minutes of brainstorming (or thinking) about what you have learned. You will be doing some short exercises related to the chapter you have just read.

What you will need to complete this task:

- A lined notebook
- A pen or pencil

Set a timer for ten minutes. Sit for a moment and think about all the things you enjoy doing in your life. Expand your mind. Think about occupations or careers you have questions about. Think about the jobs you think are cool, or jobs you might want to learn more about.

Now, don't think about what education might be required for you to do those jobs. Just think about the jobs you know or think you might enjoy.

For example, don't have negative thoughts like, "Oh, I could never learn to do that!" Just dream your favorite dreams. Like, maybe you want to be a designer of rocket ships to Mars. You could put that on your list. Or maybe you want to be a zookeeper, or a beekeeper! Or maybe you want to trek through the jungles of Africa, studying all the plants. Maybe you want to see if you can find a plant no one else has found yet.[7] Don't say, "That's impossible, there are no new plants!" Because yes, there are, and here's the proof! ". . .South African botanist, Brian du Preez (29), has discovered a beautiful new species from the Iridaceae family high up in the Langeberg Mountains of the Western Cape, South Africa."[8]

Can you just picture yourself with your backpack on your back, your safari hat pulled down over your eyes, as you trek through the jungle in South Africa with a machete in your hand, looking for new species of plants? If that picture comes in sharp and clear and sounds exciting to you, maybe you should put *botanist* on your career list.

Put at least 5 types of jobs/careers on your list. You can write down more if you want to. In fact, write as many dream jobs as you want.

Chapter Two

You Are the Coach

Did you ever think that YOU are the coach of your own life? Think about it for a moment. Who's the person you are always with? Yep, you! You make the choices for yourself. You are the one who has to weigh the pros and cons of everything you decide to do.

What does it mean to be your own coach? What skills do you need?

- Listen to your heart and your own mind. What do you need? What do you want?
- Be always curious . . . and then find the answers or info you need to satisfy that curiosity to the best of your ability.
- Explore! Make sure what you are exploring cannot hurt you or others. Don't be afraid to sign up for that field trip to the

planetarium, even if your friends aren't going. Venture forth into unknown territory. Take an elective class which you normally would not choose—like maybe chorus and drama.

- Learn from your setbacks. There are NO mistakes in life—only learning experiences of what to do or what not to do to benefit you. When something doesn't go the way you thought it should, figure out the *why. Why did it not go as planned?*[1]

- Be your own best friend. Yes, you may have many friends, but not one of those friends is going to be with you every second of your life, but you are going to be with you from here to eternity!

Yes, at your age, your friends DO have a lot of say in your life, but in the end, you make the final decisions based on YOUR knowledge, and based on you being the coach of your own life. That's why parents always use that old saying, "If Tommy jumps off a bridge, are you going to jump off a bridge, too?" Well, sometimes, when you are your age, the answer might be "yes" because, hey, friends are very important, right? One would hope you would take a moment to gauge if the drop off that bridge is too steep, and you might break your neck when you hit the water, or maybe you would have to hike down there to the river's edge to see if the water is only a foot deep.

Obstacle Course

Some decisions you must make yourself, even if Tommy and all your friends are doing it—you might have to be the one who says "no." Hey, you might be the only forward-thinking, smart one in the bunch, right? Once you realize YOU are the coach of your own life, choices become quite a bit easier to make. In the end, you are the one who will experience the happy moments and the sad moments of your life—and the obstacles and the successes based on YOUR choices as the coach of your own life.

Yes, of course, ultimately parents and caregivers dictate the rules, but in the end, it's YOU who decides whether you are going to follow those rules which have been given to you. It's all about choice.

So Many Choices

You have continued to read this book, and that is a very good thing! One could say, "a very good choice." You have already realized that you are the coach of your own life. You call the plays. You make the final decisions. Your life will always be filled with choices. Some of your decisions might affect your entire life, so they deserve to be given some deeper thought. Of course, most of your friends might not even be considering what they need to do to prepare for their future—perhaps they're just coasting along, running zigzags across the playing field, but are they gaining any ground? Probably not. (You probably are the only one who has the ball, right?)

Becoming the coach of your own life means you realize that goals and dreams are important. You wrote down a list of future jobs you think you might enjoy doing or learning more about. Nowadays, there aren't just *jobs for men* or *jobs for women.* This is a magical time to be a young person because you can decide to follow any path you want to. There may be careers you haven't even thought of. *Would you like to be a graphic designer? Would you like to design clothes? Do you think becoming a news anchor or a journalist might be interesting? How about a mechanic? What about owning your own business, like a baker? Or a butcher? Does becoming a race car driver get your blood surging?* Maybe you yearn for the spotlight in life and want to be a movie star.

What are the careers of the future which are prominent right now? Home health, chefs, software developers, nurses, medicine, animal caretakers, security analysts, truck drivers, welders, translators, hospital machine repair, physical therapists, teachers, Uber drivers, AI, and sales leaders are all careers which are trending now.

Investigate the Possibilities

No matter how old you are right this moment, no matter what grade you are in school, it isn't too early to investigate some of the jobs you like, and perhaps, narrow in on the skills you might need to pursue that path. Just like a musician probably needs to start learning about music fairly early on in life, an athlete generally starts at an early age, as well. Yet, there are fundamental skills that are necessary just to get into the game of life, no matter which path you choose to follow!

Just like that board game originally created in 1860 by Milton Bradley as *The Checkered Game of Life*, and now manufactured by Hasbro called *Life©*, before you can even BEGIN to play that game, you have to pick your car marker and the character you are going to be, and put yourself into your chosen car. Then, you begin to decide important questions like: *Will I go to college or not?* Then, you decide what you want to be. Some professions make more money than others, but they have steps you would have to complete first. A quick decision, without much thought to the career, doesn't get you a very large salary in the Hasbro game. This lower salary can limit your choices in the game, unless you are very, very lucky. Sometimes, unexpected things happen in this board game, like the birth of twins! Your odds of winning go up when you plan out your life properly in the game of Life©—just like in 'real life.' The earlier you prepare, and the more you prepare, the better your chances are for a successful, happier life.

At each age, as we get older, there are certain steps or milestones we are supposed to achieve. For example, when you were a baby, your parents couldn't wait to see you crawl, but maybe you were one of the babies who scooted backwards—hey, it happens!—or maybe you were one of those babies who never crawled—you just started walking! The point being, every healthy baby eventually makes the walking milestone, even if they did it differently than other babies, or earlier or later. They did it. The baby's parent or caregiver can check off the box: Walking.

People have their own time clock to learn new things, and to check off boxes of milestones. People also learn in many different ways. Each person is unique. You are unique. No one in this entire world is just like you. Accepting yourself as you are is one of the most important things you can do for yourself. That doesn't mean you can't change things you would like to change about yourself, but it does mean, right at this moment in time, you are okay, and you can like yourself just the way you are.

Your handicaps to learning can come in different ways, as well. Let's say you learn math skills by watching a teacher explain the steps on the board. Perhaps you like to see all the numbers lined up, and the steps in order on the board, but maybe you have a teacher who just explains, but doesn't illustrate, or maybe a teacher who says, "read page seven," and you haven't even digested page two yet. Many students begin to get gaps in their education when they can't learn in their best mode or *style* of learning.[10]

Years ago, it wasn't so important that young students began to focus on what they wanted to do as their career in the future. In fact, in those days, boys and girls were rather limited in their choices by their circumstances in life, and by virtue of being born a girl or a boy. In today's modern society, there is so much information that it really helps if a student can begin to identify where their interests and talents might lie early on in their educational path. It's much easier to define what the goals are and identify what objectives it might be necessary to obtain to reach those goals.

What is a goal? Well, in sports you know a goal means you score some points. Points are a good thing in sports! A goal in life is a bit different. Perhaps a better word for a life goal might be the word 'destination.' A destination is where you want to end up at the end of a journey. In your education the 'destination' might be to go to the next grade in school. The destination might be to graduate high school, or if you are fairly certain what you want to do in your life, you might even be thinking of graduating college, or perhaps attending a special trade school and getting a certificate which allows you to practice a certain trade. Hardly anyone has a goal in first, second, or third grade, but by fourth grade, you may start to know how you feel about certain jobs in the world. Maybe you like what your mom or dad does as their career, and you want to try it out, or you see a special YouTube video which excites you enough to want to be an entrepreneur in business.

Does this mean you are locked into the career choice forever? One thing that is important to learn in your life is that *your feet aren't set in cement.* As the coach of your own life, yes, you will make some very solid decisions, but you can always choose to change your career choice. *Will there be consequences?* Perhaps. This might mean more education is needed, or you must attend a different trade school, or take a totally different life path. But remember, you are the coach of your own life, and you can change direction.

What Is an Objective, Anyhow?

Think of an objective as a steppingstone. Each objective is something you must master or learn along the path of your life. Just like in a football game, where you must first learn how to pass a football, you must follow certain steps in your life to get you to any goal you choose. If you leave out some of these *steppingstones,* or objectives, you might fall into the river of life and have a difficult time swimming back to the shore! Steppingstones ARE important!

In each grade in school there are objectives—the steppingstones to learning something new. Most teachers don't spend time telling you this, but it just makes sense that each objective, or steppingstone, must be tackled successfully before moving on to the next one. For example, if you didn't learn what the number 5 looks like, and that it means 5 things—like 5 balls, how could you understand what 5 balls + 5 balls means? It would not make any sense to you. If you never learned what a 5 is, then it's a gap in your education, and you must go back and learn to recognize numbers. Steppingstones, or objectives, cannot be skipped or you end up with gaps in your learning!

So, just as an example, writing one of your goals might be: "Learn everything about the number five."

One of your objectives, or steppingstones, to achieve that goal might be: "I will learn to count five marbles."

Now, you have a fairly good idea what a goal is and what an objective is.

If you feel ambitious, you could write out some goals for yourself for this school year. Most students have a fairly good idea where their educational gaps might be. For example, if you keep missing a ton of words on your spelling tests, and failing the spelling quizzes, you might need some new ways to learn how to spell words. Some people call the subject of spelling their "Achilles' heel." *What is an Achilles' heel?* It's a weakness, in this case, in their education, or their 'gap.' (*Achilles* was a mythical Greek hero who could only be killed or wounded by someone injuring the heel of his foot.)

Tackle the Gaps!

Some students have gaps in mathematics, some have gaps in reading, and some never quite got their penmanship down, so no one can read their printing or cursive writing. Gaps are NOT failures. Either you weren't quite ready to learn the concept the first time round because you didn't have the eye-brain-to-hand—or the coordination—skills back then, or you needed to learn the concept in a different way, through another mode of learning. Or maybe you were so disinterested at that time, you just tuned out, and now you need to tune back in. Let's be honest, some classes are just plain boring, and though *tuning out* shouldn't be an option, sometimes students take that path. The result is that they end up with a *gap*. For example, you can't do division if you haven't learned your multiplication tables.

When you think about your goals, and when you start to write them down in your notebook, try to list the gaps you know you may have in your education. After you get these gaps identified and written down, you are going to feel so much better because now they are in front of you. You can take the steps to fill in the gaps! It's like finding a crack in a sidewalk and filling it up with cement. You can fill in your educational gaps once you make up your mind to just do it.

As the coach of your own life, it's important for you to realize that you do have the power to solve your own problems! You can take the right steps to develop the objectives—or take the right steppingstones—to accomplish the task of filling in any gaps you may have in your education.

Steps for you to take:

1. Identify some of your goals in life. (One might be to make your bed in the morning before school.)

2. Identify your educational gaps.

3. List some of the steps or objectives you will have to take to reach your goals. (The objective for *making your bed* would be to make the bed as soon as you get out of it!)

4. List some of the steps or objectives you will have to take to fill in your educational gaps.

Suggested Solutions:

1. Do you need to watch some teaching YouTube videos on the subjects you don't quite understand?

2. Do you need to tell your teacher, your parents, or your caregiver that you want a tutor to help you with learning a certain concept?

3. Can you read a book which might clarify what you don't understand?

4. Would a summer school class help fill in the gaps you have identified?

5. Is there a student in your class who understands the concept and could help you to understand it?

6. Have you tried to learn the concept in a different "mode" to activate a different part of your brain which might be stronger?

You have immense brain power. In the *old days* no one told kids very much about their brains, but brains have this marvelous ability to stretch and grow. It's called *plasticity.* Brains aren't rigid. A brain can be kind of picky as to how it learns things, but the thing is, your brain is unique to you. No one in the entire world (or maybe even the universe) has a brain wired like your brain. If you figure out your own brain's way of learning, life's road will be much easier for you!

Why are we discussing brains? Well, besides being way cool, your brain is a *machine* that is fine-tuned to help you learn new concepts—if you understand HOW to put information into it. For example, let's say that your brain likes to touch and feel things before it begins to learn them and file them in your *forever storage spot.* This means that before your brain could store the concept of the number five so that you would understand it, perhaps you would have to *feel* the five marbles. Maybe you might have to roll them around, feel how smooth they are, or pick each one up and put it into a circle, and *see them all together in that circle.* Then, your brain would make a nice, new, fresh connection, which is called a synapse, kind of like snap, crackle, pop—because it does have an electrical spark. And once that happens, your brain says, "Wow, I get it! That's the number 5!" The brain then stores that knowledge of the number five for you to use over and over again.

Brains have preferences. A brain wants to store what you learn, but because each person learns in their own way, due to their brain's preference, your brain won't store any information until you deliver it to your brain in the way it wants. Sounds funny, huh? Or maybe a little stubborn, since the brain wants what it wants in its own way! It's like when you want chocolate ice cream instead of vanilla—your brain has its own preference for learning new things.

What Type of Learning Style Does Your Brain Use?

These are the main styles of learning for most brains. Some brains combine some of the styles. When you figure out your brain's learning style, it makes it SO much easier for you to learn new things and new concepts! Wow! Who knew, right?

Visual Learner Brain. This just means your brain likes to SEE things and OBSERVE stuff before it can store what it is learning. Sometimes, a *visual learning brain* can learn from just reading a book, especially if the book has pictures. In spelling, sometimes finding little words inside the big word also can help you learn to spell a word. Circle the little words inside the big word with different color markers.

An example of this is the word: markers. You might circle Mark (like a boy's name), and you could *think*, "Mark got on an ark." You can make up any little phrase or aid to help you remember how to spell *marker*.

Auditory Learner Brain. This means your brain wants to HEAR stuff. This type of brain learning likes to listen to how to do something. Sometimes, this type of brain learning wants to talk about what it's learning. You might even have the type of brain that just can't concentrate and store information if it hears too much noise in a classroom. Auditory learner brain can sometimes hear a bird chirping outside the classroom as if it is sitting on his shoulder singing! You might hear the student two rows back discussing their trip to the zoo, and it distracts your brain so much, you just can't HEAR what you must learn. Ear muffs or headphones sometimes help these types of students' brains focus on what is being taught.

Tactile Learning Brain. This type of brain wants you to touch things before it can store the information for you. If you take five blocks and stack them, this type of brain says, *yes! I get the number 5 now!* This type of brain also likes to draw things sometimes, and that helps this type of brain store what you are learning.

Sometimes, drawing a line around the letters of a spelling word helps this brain picture how a word is spelled, but certainly, using your finger to draw the word in the sand might help, or maybe go outside and squirt your spelling words onto the cement or a fence with a squirt bottle. Try different ways to please this type of tactile learning brain. You could even make sandpaper letters and spell your spelling words with the sandpaper, and then FEEL how to spell the words, tracing your finger on the letters. You can experiment with what works best for this type of brain.

Kinesthetic Learning Brain. Most young boys benefit from some type of kinesthetic learning. This is learning through MOVEMENT. Knowing when you need to move around is very important in most boys' learning (and some girls'). Many young gentlemen need a "walkabout" every forty minutes or so. *Are you one of these young fellows who would benefit from a walkabout?* This is why some boys ask to "go to the restroom" so often during the classroom day. It isn't necessarily that they need to go to the bathroom—what they really crave is a "walk-about." *Do you begin to fidget and wiggle when* *you must sit too long?* A wise teacher always allows these "walkabouts" or builds them into the lesson plan. Standing up and jumping or running in place every forty minutes REALLY helps a kinesthetic brain! Clapping! Jumping! Stretching! A kinesthetic brain is VERY happy when these are built into the curriculum day!

If you think you might benefit from a walkabout or two built into your day, speak with your teacher. If they won't listen, speak to your counselor, your parents, or your caregiver about it. A walkabout built into your day might just be the answer to helping you fill in the gaps in your education, as well as helping you not get even more gaps as you go along. Movement helps many young boys (and older adult men, too) be able to concentrate on a task at hand. You can also jump rope while reciting your times tables or spelling your spelling words. Movement activates a different part of the brain, and this might help you learn.

Learn to recognize which learning mode your brain responds to best. Be a GREAT coach for yourself!

Storytime: There was a first-grade teacher who designed an alphabet, and later, a vowel game, where students spelled words only with movement and phonics—outside of the classroom. These first-grade students learned to read chapter books with no pictures by December, when school had just started in September! The students came into first grade not knowing how to read at all, and by December, they were excellent readers! They read the first book of *The Boxcar Children* by Gertrude Chandler.[11]

When you understand your own brain's learning style, it's easier for you to be the best coach of your own life that you can be. You can even brainstorm ideas to help you learn in new ways. Some students even think of ways to put scents into their learning, so they can SMELL the solution. This sounds funny to most people, but as the coach of your own life, it's important for you to investigate and learn how your brain learns best, and what techniques will make learning easier for YOU. *Do you need headphones to block the noise in the classroom to be able to write? Do you need a 'private office' of a cardboard carrell around your desk so you can't see the rest of the classroom, and it won't distract you?* Some teachers put a stack of cardboard carrels in the front of their classrooms so any student who feels they need a little privacy can grab one and use it as a "private office" at their desk.

Helmet & Knee Pad Time

Set your timer for 10 minutes.

What you will need to complete this task:

- Lined notebook
- Pen or pencil
- Access to the Internet

Here is the list of learning styles of most brains. Decide which ones you think your brain utilizes to learn. Write all of them down in your notebook.

1. Tactile-Touch
2. Kinesthetic-Movement
3. Visual-See
4. Auditory-Hear
5. Smell-Scents

Brainstorm quickly what you could do in each mode of learning you wrote down, for example: "Study your spelling words," or "Learn a new math concept."

Chapter Three

You Are a Great Kid, but Who Are You, Really?

You look at yourself in the mirror every day, but do you know who you really are? *Do you know anything about your personality? What is a personality, anyhow?*

All humans have some type of personality, but did you know there are different kinds of personalities?

A personality is how you think and what you do when you are thinking, then, add in your emotions, and it all comes together to make you who you are. For example, if your best friend asks to borrow your brand-new video game, *how do you respond?* Some personalities love to share, and these people share immediately. Other personalities don't enjoy sharing, and they are more cautious. *What would you do? Would you just smile and hand over your new game? Would you let your friend borrow it, but give them some rules for using your video game? Would you shout, "No way!"* Maybe the last time you loaned out your favorite game a friend broke it, and now you are more cautious. Maybe you saved your allowance for months and had to do all kinds of odd jobs to earn enough money to buy it, and now the video game is precious to you.

Sometimes, there are experiences like these in your life which shape your personality in one way or another. Your personality is unique and special to you, just like your brain is unique and special. Personality is a part of your brain, too. Your personality can even change as you get older.[12]

Your personality gives you certain things called 'traits." *What are traits?* If you are the kind of person who is very loyal and you stand by your family or friends, that is the trait of loyalty. If you believe your room must be perfect, everything folded and put away, clothes on hangers, everything in its place—that is the trait of trying to make things "perfect" called perfectionism. If you enjoy lots of attention, or maybe you even act out in class so everyone looks at you or laughs at what you do, you might have an extroverted personality trait. This means you enjoy when the focus is on you. You might even like to be the center of attention at a party, even if it isn't your party!

Personality also includes a person's character. Your character is the code you live by. For example, you may believe that you should never tell a lie. That is an ethical code. You may believe that it's important to share everything you have with others—that might be a part of your core beliefs. Core beliefs are essentially the rules you have for yourself. You are the coach in your life. You can make the rules that you live by and not break. Teachers, parents, and caregivers often make rules for you to live by, but these aren't your character codes.

You might pick up some of your parents' core beliefs, like not stealing, but you also build your own core beliefs as the coach of your own life.

What Are Your Core Beliefs?

Do you ever think about what your core beliefs might be? Core beliefs can even incorporate religious beliefs, or your belief toward other people and their beliefs. Maybe your core belief is that you must tolerate and respect the beliefs of others. Maybe you believe you must always be kind to other people, no matter how they treat you. All of these beliefs are a part of who you are.

Yourself in the Mirror

When you stare at yourself in the mirror and ask, *who am I?* you might not be able to see your core beliefs, but your core beliefs exist within you, they are a part of who you are. As you get older, you will begin to understand more and more about who you are. Young people have plenty of time to figure that out.

When you look in the mirror, you will begin to see the person you really are, instead of just seeing yourself in terms of *your father's son, or your mother's son, or as a brother, or a good student, or a not-so-good student.* You will begin to understand if you are an optimistic person—one who believes that most of the time, good things happen, or a pessimistic person—one who consistently sees the downside of things that are happening in your life. You will begin to discover that you are either a person who enjoys being with people, or who prefers being alone, or with just one or two friends.

Your confidence will become stronger as you learn more and more about being the coach of your own life. When you feel you have more control over your own life, and, therefore, most of your choices, your confidence will continue to grow. You will believe more and more in yourself and your abilities.

Only you will know if you will become a generous person, or if you are a fair and loyal person. You will discover if you have creative talents in science or mathematics, or maybe in photography, or dancing, or any other of the arts. Your personality will grow and mature as you pluck out the things in life that you enjoy most and excel in.

Your Temperament

Each human born is also born with a temperament. This means if someone squirts you with cold water from the hose you might react in certain predictable ways. You might laugh, or you might scream at them. Temperament is not learned. Temperament is biologically a part of you from the moment you are born. This is where you hear people say, "Oh, he's a cool head," or "Don't push his buttons, he's a hot head," or "This baby is amazing, he can sleep anywhere; he is so easy-going." Even dogs are born with a type of temperament. "It's a gentle dog," and "It's an aggressive dog," might be said to describe a dog's temperament.

Humans can have temperaments that make them gentle and kind or aggressive and quick to anger. *Do you know what type of temperament you have?*

Some people may have to learn to control their temperament. Even if they *feel* like punching someone, they may have to learn that it's not appropriate behavior. Even if they *feel* they deserve those new tennis shoes they see on the store shelf, they can't just walk into a store and steal them. *Do you ever feel like you must control your temperament? What steps do you take to help you control your temperament?*

Knowing your temperament can help you have a more satisfying and happy life. There are four main types of temperaments in humans. These are rather large words which you don't have to memorize, but it's good for you to hear the words, and perhaps your brain will place them in your memory bank for later.

Sanguine is one type of temperament. This is a genuine, warm, kind temperament. A person with this type of temperament believes that mostly good things happen in life. This type of temperament means that the person will be more outgoing and enjoy social gatherings. People might even label them a 'peaceful person.' *Do you see yourself as a peaceful person? Are you generally warm and kind to others? Are you the peacemaker when your friends are arguing?*

Phlegmatic is the second type of temperament. When this word is first learned, thinking of a slimy snail as it's moving in its phlegm very slowly, helps to remember the word. This temperament takes its time. Generally, a person with this temperament is slower, relaxed, and it takes a lot going on around them before this type of temperament gets excited or upset. *When the orange juice glass flips over, do you just calmly get a paper towel and wipe it up, or do you lose your cool? If you get a lower grade on a test, do you just accept it and move on?*

Melancholic is the third type of temperament. A person with this temperament might sit back and watch others in action. This temperament tends to analyze what they see or categorize it. They might talk about "plan A or plan B" as other choices when they analyze. They definitely have opinions. They think about things of the past with warmth—sometimes thinking it was better then instead of now. *Do you often have to have the answer* *to 'why' something is happening or 'why' it's important? Do you want to know all the options before you make any choices? Are you quick to judge others?*

Choleric is the fourth type of temperament. This temperament jumps to conclusions, but it also jumps into action when something needing action occurs. The downside of this temperament is that the person with this temperament can be a bit irritable and grouchy, kind of like they need a nap.[13]

Do you see your temperament on this list? Many people have a combination of these temperaments. Knowing your temperament can help you to know a little bit more about who you are, and why you react to certain things that happen in your life, and the way you react.

Helmet & Knee Pad Time

Set your timer for ten minutes.

What you will need for this task:

- Lined notebook
- Pen/Pencil
- Access to a computer for YouTube

- List what you believe are your temperament traits.
- For fun, and also for some more insight as to who you are, take this quick six-minute quiz to learn more about yourself and your personality.[3]

Chapter Four

The "Prove It" Principle

Have you ever heard your inner voice? For some people, these are thoughts they hear in their head telling them to do something or not do something; thoughts that say, this is right or that is wrong. Some people call it 'little angels on my shoulder' for positive thoughts and 'the devil on my shoulder' for negative thoughts. When you are with your friends, it might be the friend who says to you, "Yah, so prove it!" to some comment you have made.

The most influential person in your life is YOU. Remember, you are the coach of your own life. You are the one who can decide whether to do something or not do it. The only person you ever need to prove anything to is YOURSELF.

The Hypothesis

Do you remember what the definition of a hypothesis is? A hypothesis is when you make a guess about something based on the information you have, which may not be all the information available to you. The hypothesis is basically just a beginning point—the guess—and often requires you to keep digging to find more information before you can work out if the hypothesis is correct. Sometimes, a hypothesis is wrong, so you have to think again.

Right now, you can make a hypothesis about what your future career is going to be. You can base your hypothesis on:

- Things you enjoy at your age right this moment
- The knowledge of that career you have already developed, which is probably limited
- The education you have obtained thus far
- Your lack of knowledge about the many other careers which are available

You are at the stage of your life where you can make your hypothesis. But you must also understand that it will take a lot more investigation into all possibilities before you can come to a final decision.

Remember, you don't have to prove anything to anyone, except yourself, right now.

This is a very freeing thought. Let's say your dad loved playing football at your age; now, he may want you to try out for the team. But perhaps you don't enjoy football. Perhaps you want to try out for the tennis team instead, or work on the school newspaper. *Does this mean you have to argue with your father?* No, it means you must be *honest* with your father, no matter how difficult that may be. You see, sometimes parents and caregivers don't realize they are pushing their child into things because they themselves enjoy them. But that means they aren't thinking about what their child enjoys or doesn't enjoy. Truthfully, even if they tend to do this, most parents and caregivers don't want to hurt or harm you by it. They really believe that something was good for them, so it should be good for you, as well. Just tell them honestly how you feel. You don't have to say, "I hate football!" You can say instead, "Dad, football is great, but I want to play tennis." Now, this is not to say that some parents or caregivers still might come back with something hurtful, but building your character is a good thing, too. You can hear their words, acknowledge them, and still repeat your desire: "I hear what you are saying, Dad, but I am going to work on the school newspaper instead." This is NOT easy for some children. A parent or caregiver can see this as a negative comment and a threat to their control over their child. It's up to you to help soften this response to your parent, so it doesn't get blown out of proportion. *How can you do that?* You could say something like, "Dad, I still want to go to the games with you! That will be a lot of fun."

Speaking to an Adult

It's sometimes difficult for a young person to make their desires and dreams known to adults, especially adults in authority. Your personality and your temperament can make it even more difficult for you to speak out for yourself, but your life is important. Your choices are important. You are the coach of your own life. Yes, it helps to be respectful towards your parents, caregiver, and your teachers, however, you must also respect who you are, who you are becoming, and the dreams you may have which are yours to pursue.

Storytime: There once was a young man who was born into a family of 4 brothers and 3 sisters. They lived on a farm in Indiana. The young man was brilliant. He loved math. He loved to read. He did not like cows, chickens, pigs, alfalfa, corn, and wheat! The parents needed the boys help their father on the farm, and the girls helped the mother in the house. But this young man just wanted to read. He wanted to learn more about the world. His father didn't understand him. He often asked him, "Why can't you be like your other brothers? This farm will be yours one day, and you have to learn how to farm." So, he was a very unhappy young man. His father was a man with a very strong personality. He was afraid to speak to his father about his own desire to go to college to become an engineer. Then, one day, the young man had an idea. His father put him on the tractor to plow the rows. Back and forth, back and forth he went. So, he put the book he was reading on the steering wheel of the tractor, so he could read it while he plowed, and he got lost in his reading. The rows he plowed were crooked and wiggled back and forth, instead of being straight. Then, he actually hit the fence with the tractor! His father was so upset, he never put his son on a tractor again!

Certainly, the young man got his father's attention, but his father shunned him from that moment on. *Wouldn't he have had a better outcome if he'd spoken with his father about his true feelings?* Perhaps, but there is no guarantee his father would have listened. He was a very stubborn man. The young man ended up going to Purdue University, and he received his engineering degree. Though he took drastic measures, he still changed his own life for the better. His brothers all became farmers, and his sisters all married farmers. But he followed his dream.

Self-Love

You may have to change your own life for the better. *Who better than you to take care of you?* Remember, you are going to be with you to the end of your days. *What kind of coach will you be? Won't you always have your best interests at heart?* Sometimes, you may have to prove to yourself that you can do something. You may have to reach deep down inside you and pull up the will and the drive to do it. You may not have someone cheering you on. You may never get a pat on the back telling you, "Great job!" You may look around at times and realize that you are a team of ONE. In that case, it helps to understand that you are your best supporter, you are your best cheerleader, and truly, you need to love yourself, as well.

Most young people don't think loving yourself is important. However, it's probably the most important thing in life. When you love yourself, you are able to like others or love others in return. You are able to accept who you are, what you look like, and embrace your own dreams. Young boys often have a little difficulty with this. *Why?* Well, there is a lot of peer pressure at your age. It seems that some of the strongest people (sometimes, with the weakest characters) rise to the top at this time of life. Some of these fellows even turn into bullies. Now that you understand YOUR character, your temperament, and your personality, you might be able to become stronger and not give in to this peer pressure.

The thing is, peer pressure is often in the lives of humans forever. How you learn to deal with it is very important. The more you know and understand yourself and who you are, the easier it's to steer clear of peer pressure.

As the coach of your own life, you ultimately make the rules for yourself. Yes, your parents, your teachers, and society make rules, but it's ultimately

YOU who decide if you will obey them or not. *Do you do your homework without someone nagging you?* It's your choice. *Do you smoke or do drugs?* It's ultimately your choice, isn't it? *Do you do what the so-called leader in your group of friends tells you to do, or do you keep your own mind?* That's up to you, as well. You are beginning to define who you are, not what others say you should be.

Parents, caregivers, teachers, and well-meaning relatives or friends may try to sway you to one decision or another. You may not even be interested in what they say, but you want to please them, rather than follow your own dream. A singer from the 1960s, Sammy Davis, Jr. sang a song which is appropriate for almost everyone even today. His song, "I Gotta Be Me"[15] states, "What else can I be, but what I am?" So, you will always be who you are, but will you hold on to your dreams, and will you do whatever it takes to achieve them?

Never Too Early to Dream

Though many people will say it's a bit early in your life for you to prepare for your dreams and your future, the truth is, nowadays, life moves very quickly. Technology changes daily. It's not too early for you to begin to think in terms of *what do I need to do to achieve my dreams? What gaps must I fill to ensure I have a bright future of my choice. Do I accept that I can't read that well? Do I accept that I don't do math very well? Do I accept what my parents or caregivers want me to be when I grow up, or do I become what I want to become? Do I make good choices to help build a happy future for myself, or do I make rotten choices which start me down a bad path?*

In Sammy Davis, Jr.'s song he sings, "The dream that I see makes me what I am."[16] This may or may not be true, but again, if you don't have dreams, it's impossible to have any dreams come true.

The "Prove It Principle" only means that there is only one person you will ever have to prove anything to. That person is YOU.

Helmet & Knee Pad Time

Set your timer for ten minutes.

What you will need for this task:

- Lined notebook
- Pen/Pencil

- Access to a computer

In your notebook, write down a "hypothesis" of what you think might be a job that will interest you in your future. Now, open your computer and do a search for this job. In your notebook, answer these questions:

1. Does this future job have interests which you enjoy right now?

2. Will this job mean you must go to college or a trade school?

3. What classes could you take in grammar school, middle school, and high school that might prepare you to make an educated choice about this job?
   Grammar School:
   Middle School:
   High School:

4. If your school doesn't offer any classes which might help you with your choice, where could you get more information and training for this job choice?

Chapter Five

Do I Have to Choose Now?

Right now, depending on your age, you might not be pressured to choose your future job. But if you are starting high school, it would be time to begin to buckle down and focus on some specific career choices, so you can prepare. When you are in grammar school and middle school is the time when you can explore and research what type of jobs you might enjoy. Remember, finding a career you might enjoy will help make your future work a true pleasure!

Options and Rabbit Holes!

There is a television show on American TV called "Dirty Jobs."[17] What is so amazing about this show is that a man named Mike Rowe actually performs all kinds of jobs which most people never knew existed, for instance, a 'bat cave scavenger.' *Does that sound interesting to you?* This is a job where you go into a cave and gather the bat guano (poop) to be used as fertilizer. Mr. Rowe has investigated jobs like becoming a rattlesnake catcher to becoming a 'roadkill cleaner.' Unless you are willing to do a bit of investigating, or going down interesting so-called *rabbit holes*, you might miss finding a job that would pay you well and could make you very happy, depending on your personal interests, of course. Rowe introduces jobs like a 'caviar harvester,' while most kids wouldn't even know what 'caviar' is. *Do you know?* What about becoming a 'spice maker' or a 'candle maker'?

Make Time to Investigate

This is YOUR life we are discussing here, so the time you spend finding out about different types of career choices is time well spent.[18] *Did you know that in Finland a hotel chain hired someone as a professional sleeper?* The hotel wanted to know if all of its bedrooms were comfortable. The 'professional sleeper' went from hotel to hotel, to sleep in the rooms and test the beds! Who knew, right?

If you Google 'underwater pizza delivery,' guess what? You will find that job in Florida! It's an actual job for an underwater hotel.

A job for you fellows who enjoy science but don't want to get bogged down with all those formulas, would maybe to become a 'snake milker.' This is the person who milks the venomous snakes of their venom to make antidotes for snake bites. This job combines adventure, suspense, and science!

You can see now that traveling down some rabbit holes or investigating paths will be interesting, and you might just stumble on a job that makes you say, "Wow, I want to do that!" Then, you can plan your education goals to help you reach all the prerequisites needed to choose that job. *What is a prerequisite?* That's just a fancy word for all the boxes you have to check off before you can perform a particular task, in this case, the job you are interested in.

Canine Gourmet Job

Can you imagine getting paid to taste dog food? Yep, it's a real job. Probably the prerequisite is finishing high school and having a fine palate. *What does THAT mean?* That means your taste buds can fine-tune the taste of food.

These examples are just the tip of what is available in your future world of employment. This is why it's important to educate yourself on what is *out there* in the world to explore for you—before you become an adult.

Yes, it's not THAT exciting to do research about careers when there are so many other things you want to do and have to do in your life right now. The fact is, many people aren't book-learners, they know how to read, but they don't enjoy it. Maybe they like being outdoors, breathing in the fresh air, or maybe they like sitting in one place counting things. Find out who you are and find out what you like! You might have to push yourself into doing what must be done. Roll up your sleeves and just do it! Be the best coach you can be for yourself. The International Olympic Committee has listed ten qualities which make someone a great coach.[19]

These ten qualities can be modified to suit your needs as your own coach.

1. Understand and KNOW what you need to do for yourself. You can even lead others by your own example.

2. Have a genuine thirst for knowledge—dig out answers. Think about things before making a judgment or a decision.

3. Be willing to help others, and be willing to take help from others. A person doesn't have to have all the answers all the time.

4. Be excited and motivated to achieve your goals and objectives!

5. Value and respect yourself and value and respect others.

6. Utilize your words to ask questions. Communicate with others to get answers.

7. Train yourself to tune in and listen to people when they are speaking. For some people, it means making a true effort to concentrate on the other person's face and actually *listen* to what they are telling you—not being eager to just get your own point heard, but actively listening to others' opinions, questions, and needs. It also means being tuned in to your own questions and voicing those questions.

8. Practice self-discipline so you can get things done. Don't wait for the "hammer" of your

parents to come down to 'make' you do your homework or clean your room. Own up to what went wrong and vow to yourself that you can change it. Be your own prodding stick. *What does THAT mean?* It means when you are sitting playing video games, and you know you have homework to do, you push yourself to turn off the video game, and do what you need to do. A prodding stick is a poking stick generally used with livestock to get them to move into corrals or onto trucks. Some animals need a prodding stick to get moving. You are a human being with your own self-motivation. You can prod yourself into action!

9. Be a person of character. Follow your rules, even when it's difficult for you to do so. Stay as positive as you can, even when you feel defeated. Find ways to help yourself. Seek out solutions. As the coach of your own life, hold your chin high, and know that you can succeed.

10. You are in control of you. Be committed to your success. Each day, make a commitment to yourself to put forward your best effort in

whatever you are doing. Here's some more from the International Olympic Committee report: "Coaching is a 24/7, 365-days-a-year job . . . [A coach] . . . think[s] of every possible scenario . . . to perform at their best when the pressure is at its greatest."[4]

Helmet & Knee Pad Time

Set your timer for ten minutes.

What you will need for this task:

- Lined notebook
- Pen/Pencil
- Access to a computer

In this chapter you learned that there are a lot of unusual jobs in the world. Go to your computer and Google some of the unusual jobs. List three of those unusual jobs which you find interesting or think you might like to do in your notebook. Write a short note explaining each job. Write at least one sentence about why you think you might like this unusual job.

Try these Google search words:

ARIANA SMITH

Unusual Jobs

30 of the Weirdest Jobs in the World

Chapter Six

Can You Move the Goal Posts?

Technically, well, the answer is, yes. "Goal posts were on the goal line. When the NCAA moved them to the end zone's backline in 1927, the NFL followed suit. In 1933, however, the NFL adopted its own rule book and placed the goal posts back on the goal line. NFL goal posts stayed there until 1974, when they were moved to the back of the end zone."[21]

This means that, yes, you can have a goal, and then, for various reasons, change your goal, or even remove it, or postpone your goal.

How Many Goal Posts Can I Have?

Since you are the coach of your own life, you can decide how many goals you are going to make for yourself in your life. Not only that, but you can also decide what steps or objectives you are going to take to reach those goals.

In American football there were many adjustments to goals. There were problems with how long the field should be and where to put the goals, and even what they would be made of. "The solution was to shorten the end zones to ten yards deep. To accommodate this extra twenty yards, the field of play for American Football was shortened from 110 yards, which resembled more the size of a rugby field, to 100 yards. It was decided that the back line of the end zone would be considered out-of- bounds."[22]

What Is 'Out of Bounds' in Your Life?

Are there things you would not do in your life? What do you consider "out of bounds" in your future life? Do you think about the things you will do and the things you won't do? The time for this consideration is definitely BEFORE you attempt to do them. As the coach of your own life, you will sometimes have to make major decisions right in the moment, and for other decisions, you might have time to ponder and research.

For example, if all of your friends are climbing into your friend's car, the friend who just got his driver's license ahead of all of you because he is older, and you are all sneaking off to the beach instead of going to class—*What would you do?* Do you go automatically with your friends and skip school? Do you take a moment to consider what the consequences might be? Or perhaps you have already made a rule for yourself that you would not skip classes in school. Perhaps you have already decided which lines you won't cross. Some things are definitely better decided ahead of time instead of on the spur of the moment!

As you get older, as the coach of your own life, you will have to make lots of on-the-spot decisions. You must rely on your character, your wisdom, and who you have decided you want to be, to make those sometimes difficult choices. *Will you be strong enough to say "no" when you must? Will you be wise enough to say "yes" when you should?*

Life's Pitfalls

There are always positive and negative sides to the decisions anyone makes in their life. At your age, it's very difficult to slow down, and weigh the positive and negative consequences of your decisions and actions. Now, more than ever, it becomes necessary for you to think about your future. What you choose to do now, may reflect on what you are able to do in your life later. You can choose not to study for your science test, but remember, these are the 'gaps' you need to fill if you want to be a doctor or a scientist, or a chemical engineer, or a botanist, or anything having to do with science. Yes, it starts with studying for this science test, and the next science test, and the one after that, and so on.

Every single thing which you learn in school builds on the last item you learned. Learning is a progression of steps. If you find you have gaps in your education—things you didn't quite master or understand first time around—it's up to YOU, as the coach of your own life, to find a way to fill in those gaps—to learn what you did not learn.

In today's world there are a lot of solutions online, but there are also people in your life who you can speak with and get assistance from. Be pro-active. Be your own coach!

To avoid falling behind in your classes, you have to be a strong coach. You can't allow yourself to just say, "I don't need to study for the test," or "This test isn't that important anyhow," or even, "This is so horribly boring, I'm not going to do it." Remember, sometimes the things we learn in school seem to be boring, but when we are older, we look back, and we draw on some of these early lessons in our adult lives.

Consequences of Choice

For example, let's say you would like to be a firefighter. This requires you to be able to climb ladders. Maybe you decide to play football in school. *Will playing football in school help or harm your ability to become a firefighter?* [23]

"The majority of football-related injuries occur to the musculoskeletal system, most notably the lower leg, ankle, and foot."[24] If you receive an injury, there is a small percentage chance that it could impact your ability to become a firefighter. But according to Dr. Matava, "Despite the perception that the majority of football participants will eventually sustain an injury, a recent study by USA Football found that more than 90 percent of the youth players did not suffer an injury that restricted participation. Contusions were the most common injuries (35%), followed by ligament sprains (15%). Fewer than 4% of the youth players sustained a concussion."[25]

So, do you or don't you play sports?

The conclusion is that there is a slight risk of getting a sports injury which could impact your life later on, but the main takeaway is that sports are good for young people—and older people, too! It's good to get your muscles moving and fresh blood flowing and nice fresh air into your lungs. You will have the physical and psychological reward of being 'out there' playing and enjoying yourself.

Calculated Risks

As the coach of your own life, when you do your research on the jobs you think you might like to pursue, yes, you must weigh the negative and the positive sides of everything you do. This doesn't mean just sitting on the sidelines out of fear that you might "be the one" who sustains a sports injury. Sometimes, you will take a risk—like when you meet new people. *Will that new person become a loyal friend?*

In the beginning, you may not know if he or she is a true, honest, and loyal person. That person might hurt you emotionally in the end, but isn't reaching out and enjoying the new friendship important, as well? "Calculated risks" are a part of a healthy life.

Nothing you do in your life can be guaranteed to be totally safe from getting an injury—emotional or physical. However, no matter what happens in your life, you are the coach of your own life. You will weigh the good and the not-so-good of each choice you make. Life is full of *calculated risks.* These are risks that you think about, research, and after self-debate and consideration, decide if you want to go ahead with, based on your research and knowledge.

Helmet & Knee Pad Time

Set your timer for ten minutes.

What you will need for this task:

- Lined notebook
- Pen/Pencil

By now you probably are starting to think of some goals you might want to add to your list. You may even have decided that one of those jobs you researched sounds like a good choice for you. Close your eyes and take a moment to think about the things you are very good at doing. Then, write down 3 things which you think you are an expert at doing. These should be things you know how to do so well, you are sure you could teach someone else to do them. Write the 3 skills in your notebook which you feel very confident about.

Chapter Seven

Macho Man or Piano Man?

Boys can be rough and tumble, or boys can be quieter, and enjoy reading or playing the piano. *Are either of these characterizations normal or not normal?* There is no set list of things that only a boy can do or not do. Ideally, young men and boys should strive to have a balance in their lives. One study about males suggests that ". . . the attack on traditional masculinity is an attack on the very nature of men . . ."[26] To say that all boys must have an aggressive, competitive nature would not be fair. You are who you are. As the coach of your own life, it's your job to pursue greatness in your life, and for you to become everything you want to become. Rising to all the challenges life presents to you should be your ultimate goal.

Pursuing Greatness

What do you need to do to pursue greatness? Greatness is just another word for *success.* There are certain things you should be aware of which are essential when you pursue greatness for yourself:

- Motivate yourself. This sounds like an easy task, but as we said previously, prodding yourself to do what must be done isn't always easy. Some boys get in the bad habit of waiting for adults to push them to do something that needs to be done. If you find yourself doing this, you are pushing greatness away from yourself! Motivate yourself to do what you are supposed to do. Remember, your parents, caregivers, and teachers have already found their "greatness," and when you sense them nagging or pushing, it's just them wanting you to achieve YOUR greatness.

- Write out your goals and then pursue them.

- Don't give up! Be persistent and determined to be the best self-coach you can be.

- Don't talk negatively about yourself. What

you say, you may come to believe! Don't say, "I'm so stupid," or "I can never learn that," or "I am dumb in math like my father," or "I can't write well." Don't accept these negative comments about yourself, especially not if someone else is saying them to you.

- Do look in the mirror daily and affirm yourself. Don't be afraid to say things like, "You've got this!" or "I don't have to get a 100%, I just have to do my best!" or "I like myself." It may sound funny to say that about yourself, but remember, liking yourself is number one on your list of being a great coach for yourself! No put-downs of yourself!

- Follow your own passion. Learn to make yourself happy. Don't feel you have to be like everyone else. Yes, at this age, you may WANT to be like others, which is a normal thing, but hold on to your own dreams and passions, too.

- Know your strengths and use them to your advantage. *Are you good at art?* Then, volunteer for the committee at school making posters for the bake sale. *Are you good at science?* Don't be afraid to start a science fair project and enter it into the fair. Be bold and be brave.

- Always remember that there are no failures. Each time you try, and attempt to succeed at something, you learn along the way.

- Accept that every human being on earth has some weaknesses. Know what your weaknesses are, and work to compensate for them, or even work to strengthen them.

Ties and Tails

Remember, there are many different types of people in the world. There are those young men who like to have their hair combed just so, and their clothes pressed, and they want to wear the latest fashion. Then, there are young men who just throw on their T-shirts and jeans, and off they go, maybe even forgetting to comb their hair! Neither of these examples is wrong. The important thing to do is begin to understand and know yourself, and who you want to be.

What to Wear? (Can You Dress for Greatness?)

Some boys go through their school years content with that sweatshirt and jeans, but then, one day they just take a different turn. Some might call it an awakening or *dressing for success.* "A guy might look totally blah most of the time, but then one day, he walks into geometry class looking like a supermodel . . . and you wonder to yourself: *What happened? What changed?*"[27] Being trendy isn't for everyone, but some boys might feel more comfortable when they can *kind of* blend in. It's like the spots on a cheetah hiding him in the wild brush. Perhaps you want to blend in and be like your friends, so you want to dress in trendy styles which match theirs—like the cheetah. You don't have to go so far as to adopt the *supermodel theme* mentioned above, but there are styles which some boys like to follow. Just know that this is normal behavior. But try not to lose yourself in this process. Develop your own style. Develop your own likes and dislikes.

Is there anything wrong with following your group of friends or the so-called 'in-crowd'? That depends. If the *in-crowd* is marching off the cliff, probably not. But if it means following what others are wearing, again, to blend in, and to be a comfortable part of a group, it's your personal choice. You are the coach of your own life, so you will decide if you are a "trendsetter" or a "trend follower."

Some researched current "in-crowd" ideas for boys and young men:

- Leather jackets, topcoats, blazers (worn with pink dyed heads, apparently), suits
- Air Force 1's, loafers with no socks
- Bow ties, neck chains made of anything (even paperclips), rings on every finger
- Flannel shirts, beanies, graphic tees, sunglasses, cargo pants

You can probably add your favorites to this list. At your age, it's often very important for you to feel part of the group, so knowing what is "in" could be helpful. You don't 'have to' be like everyone else. You could be a person who just marches to the beat of your own drum. This just means that as the coach of your own life, there ARE infinite options to what you wear or don't wear. Dressing like your peer group or not is another one of your many choices.

Dirt Under Your Nails

This subtitle doesn't mean that you let your nails get dirty. What it does mean is that you aren't afraid to work hard for what you want or need. If you are eight years old, you probably rely on your parents for your wardrobe, which is what most boys your age do. If you are older, well, there is always the 'money factor' to think of, as well. If your parents purchase your clothes, you might not be able to keep up with the latest trends. You might even begin thinking about getting a part-time weekend job mowing lawns, or perhaps babysitting in the neighborhood, or bagging groceries at the supermarket. It never hurts to get a little *dirt under your nails* working for something you would like. At eight years old you can still volunteer for jobs around the house—and maybe negotiate some kind of *deal* for that jacket or tennis shoes you want.

At this point in your life, your responsibilities, and your abilities, change almost daily. You might even be asking your parents or caregivers for more freedom to do what you enjoy doing. But remember, with more freedom comes more responsibility.

Boys who are interested in just running around the track, jumping hurdles, playing football and basketball, and just getting their homework done, probably don't think so much about all these trendy things. But if you do, just know that it's absolutely normal for you to want to dress like your peers at this age, blending in, like the cheetah in the jungle.

Your parents or caregivers might not have enough money in their budget for the trendy things you want, so that would be a motivator for you to seek out a way to make extra money beyond your allowance, or perhaps, you don't even GET an allowance. As you get older, finances become more and more important in your life.

Storytime: There once was a young fella, about twelve, who liked being trendy. He wasn't much into sports, other than he liked to jog and skateboard. He saw this "look" in a movie he liked. None of his friends were wearing anything that looked like it, but he decided he was going to start wearing an ascot. "An ascot is a neckwear accessory consisting of two long, wide wings connected by a slim band, all made of fabric. The wings are usually the same size, and they constitute the decorative element of the article, while the band is intended to sit upon the neck and secure the wings."[28] This young fella started wearing the ascot in middle school. At first, the other boys made fun of him, and girls stared at him, but he had seen the style in a history book, and he liked it. It became his 'signature look' all the way through college. His friends started wearing ascots, too. He was a trendsetter. He is still wearing ascots—even when no one else does!

However, sometimes, it's difficult becoming different or doing something different than everyone else. But when you begin to coach yourself into becoming who you want to be, it becomes easier and easier to just be your own person. Sometimes, adults call this ability to just shake off the comments or jokes of others *"learning how to have a thicker skin."* The idea behind this is that you are strong enough to be your own person, even under peer pressure. This is especially beneficial to you when your peers or friends decide to do something you don't agree with. When you have a *thicker skin,* it means it won't bother you *as much* to hear people make negative comments about what you wear, what you do (like doing your homework instead of playing), or what rules you have decided to adopt as your rules of character.

Becoming You

Who are you? Are you the guy who helps someone carry a big stack of books down the hallway at school without being asked? Are you the guy who is there for your friends when they need you? Sometimes, a fella wants to be alone, but if you find you are alone most of the time, it's time for your 'coach self' to prod you into joining some groups at school. Maybe join the swim team, or take a cooking class, or join a book club. Prod yourself out of your comfort zone so you can begin to develop another part of yourself. *Becoming you* means you are working to become your best self.

Invest time in your bro-friendships. Share your ideas. Share your knowledge.

"...Boys learn best in small groups through big conversations and hands-on projects."[29] When you know and understand this, you can be a positive influence on your friends. Be a true friend by setting a good example. Also, something most boys don't understand is that it's VERY important to tell someone when you need help. This is especially important when you begin to realize you have gaps which are beginning to cause issues with your learning in school. Look around you. Are there younger boys who might look up to you as their mentor? Maybe you have the knowledge to help them with their educational gaps.

Helmet & Knee Pad Time

Set your timer for ten minutes.

What you will need for this task:

- Lined notebook
- Pen/Pencil

Hopefully, you are beginning to develop some principles and rules which you intend to live by in your life, no matter what. Take a moment to think what those principles or rules might be. These are your own standards that you tell yourself that you won't break. Perhaps one of them is that you will respect others and yourself.

Write down at least three of the principles you won't compromise in your life—three standards or rules which you believe are important that you will never break or breach.

Chapter Eight

Rocket to the Moon

Do you ever think about how it would be to get on a rocket and travel to the moon? Or *do you think about how it would be to design the next best mode of transportation?* People in history like Orville and Wilbur Wright dreamed about flying in an airplane. Then, they tried to do it. When you allow your mind to dream, there is an abundance of things you could accomplish in your future.

Note to self: It's difficult to dream when my nose is always in a video game or I'm texting. *Where is the place where you find yourself able to daydream? Do you go there to dream and think?* Some people ride their bicycle into the wind and that's where their great thoughts come. Other people go on a hike and breathe in nature and that is where their great thoughts come. *Do you have a place where your great* *thoughts flow?* It's very important to nurture those dream thoughts.

For example, there have been scientists and other people who have had the dream of building a tunnel from New York City to London. This thought is in the "dream-thought" stage. ". . .The main barriers to constructing such a tunnel are the costs, first estimated $88–175 billion, now updated to $1–20 trillion, as well as limits of current materials science."[30] It will be a young person, like you, who will figure out how to cut the costs for that tunnel, so it can be built. There will also be a young person, like you, who will figure out the safest and fastest way to move through that tunnel.

The Challenges—What I Need to Know

You have learned a little bit about what *gaps in your education* are. Generally, humans think they have all the time in the world to do what they want to do, especially young boys. However, the reality is that this is the time, right this moment, for you to begin to fill in your gaps.

The first thing to do is identify the gaps, which, hopefully, you have already done.

Then, you tackle filling in the gaps one at a time. You know what subjects you find hardest. *Are you struggling in science? Have you been lost since fractions started? Do you have to keep repeatedly reading the same sentence because you have trouble reading?*

There are academic solutions to all of these issues. But besides that, if there are learning issues which do not seem to have solutions, teachers and counselors can identify remedies for learning issues. Earlier in this book, we discussed different modes of learning.

Yet, one thing which is very important is to have a true 'vision' of what you want. *How can you develop your 'vision'?* That's difficult to say. Some people start to have a vision naturally; it's born into them. Whereas other people need to develop their focus to achieve what they want in life. [31] *Do you have a vision for your life that shows you where you want to be or who you want to be in your future?* "When children have vision, they can make decisions in the context of how their choices will affect their future desires. Without vision, every decision is a coin toss, where thoughts about the potential consequences or ramifications aren't present, and obviously cannot be weighed . . ."[32]

What does this mean? Basically, it means what you already know—without a dream or a *vision for your future,* you aren't going to be able to achieve it. *How can you make the right decisions without knowledge of what you might want?* You won't know which classes you should concentrate on. You won't know what books to read or which web addresses will have more of the right information.

Back to the Issue of Educational Gaps

Gaps destroy dreams. That's a fact.

So, gaps in your education should not be ignored. Or rather, you can ignore them, but you won't be able to pursue your true vision. Gaps ALWAYS get in the way.

It's easy to push this all to the back of your mind and ignore it.

Your mind right now might be on sports, your buds, and yes, perhaps a certain person who has caught your eye, too. All of these are important things to boys your age. It's tempting to want to push thoughts about your gaps in mathematics, gaps in reading skills, gaps in writing skills, or gaps in science to the back of your mind. Maybe you want to bury these thoughts, so you don't have to think about them at all. However, just like those murder mysteries in books or on TV, someone always digs up the information eventually—and eventually, when you are ready to venture forth into your career or tackle some challenge you want to achieve, your gap will be dug up. If you want to be a real estate agent but never learned about percentages, it will be difficult to become a real estate agent. *Why?* Because when they are selling houses, real estate agents are always figuring out the percentage of sales, the percentage of commissions, and necessary things related to those percentages.

It's important for you to realize that, yes, you can make the choice to push all of this to the back of your mind for later. You can choose to forget about it altogether, as long as you are aware that you might not have your dream come true—or ever achieve your vision.

It's extremely important for you to realize that when you ignore fixing your gaps, it's like tying your hands and hobbling your feet. Will you hop up the ladder to become an airplane pilot? A bit difficult with hobbled feet, right? Will you become a world-renowned baker if you can't figure out fractions? Will you be the best mechanic in your town? Probably not, if you don't learn the metric system, or know how to convert your tools to the metric system to fix an engine made in Europe. The list could go on and on. Dreams can easily die if you do not nurture them, as you would a plant.

Developing your 'vision' is so important for your future success. "See" yourself in your mind's eye doing what you want to do in your future life. Then, you can make sure you check all the boxes to achieve that vision.

Helmet & Knee Pad Time

Set your timer for ten minutes.

What you will need for this task:

- Lined notebook
- Pen/Pencil

Developing your 'vision' doesn't mean you cannot change or adjust it, or even fine-tune it, as you go along in your life. Take a few moments to think about the future. What type of job do you 'see' yourself doing in your future?

Write this job in your notebook.

Think about the skills you can begin developing right now which you might need to do that job in the future.

Write down two skills you believe you would probably need but feel you need to improve. *Would you say you have gaps in these skills or areas in your current education?*

Write down a solution for each of these two gaps which you can begin to address today.

Chapter Nine

Getting Down to Brass Tacks

- Do you have a dream or vision?
  It doesn't have to be the dream of *what you are going to be when you grow up.* It CAN be that dream, or it can just be another dream of yours, like being picked as the captain of the debate team, or the lead in the school play, or making the touchdown that wins the game.

- Can you imagine yourself accomplishing this dream or vision?

- Can you imagine the skills you might need to accomplish this dream, or what you might have to do to make it a dream come true? Sometimes, knowing the step you need to accomplish ahead of time will help you achieve a dream come true.

- Are you able to focus on a job you really would like to do in your future? Is there someone you know, or would like to know, who can tell you about that job? When you focus on the future, you can do things to help make it come true. You can write a letter or an email to someone who does the job and ask them to tell you about it. They can tell you what they had to learn to get their job. Of course, you can always look up the job on the Internet and go down the rabbit holes to learn about it.

- What steps do you think you might need to be able to do this job well?

- Do you think there are some steps that are universal for most jobs in the future? *Universal* means something that is applicable to everyone, literally, everyone in the universe. So, there are some skills you need to do any job. Some universal skills you need to learn for most employment might be:

1. Learning how to read

2. Learning how to take notes and highlight important items
3. Learning how to write
4. Learning numbers and basic math (addition, subtraction, multiplication, division, fractions, decimals, measurements)
5. Learning how to keep records (like a checkbook)
6. Learning time management
7. Learning interpersonal skills—which is learning how to get along with other people, speaking with others, explaining your opinion
8. Learning communication skills—this isn't just talking, but listening too, and active listening and sharing

It's important to know something about where you are heading and, hopefully, how to get there. It's also important to learn more about some of the career paths you might have found interesting. Your goal posts are set and solid for now. But remember, just as the posts on the football field have been moved and changed throughout the years, your life goal posts can also be changed!

A Leg-Up With Technology

Managing your time and your money well are two important skills which can help you get organized. The Internet has a wealth of information to help you do this successfully.

There are many charts to print out, or apps for your phone to help you. There are apps to help you keep track of homework or chores, for instance. There are apps to help you keep track of what you earn too.

Your parents can even send your allowance directly to your bank account. That way, you can learn how to manage your money. There are apps which can help you save, invest, and give to others.[33] This isn't such a novel idea, though, today, it has the modern twist of computers. However, in the 1960s, people from the banks went into grammar schools and started savings programs with the students. Students would put money in their bank envelopes each week to turn in to the bank for their savings each Friday. This helped young people establish the habit of saving some of their earnings for the future. Students would just write out their deposit slips and put them in their 'bank bag,' which was then given to the banker when they came in to collect the students' bags. Students learned valuable skills like filling out their deposit slips and the habit of saving for the future. Times have changed, and deposit slips and checkbooks are hardly used today—most of us do our banking online. However, the same money management skills apply, and, as the coach of your life, you can benefit from learning them.

In fact, any good habits you learn now can be very beneficial to you later.

- Good savings habits
- Good cleaning habits
- Good time management habits
- And yes, even good health and hygiene habits

No Couch Potatoes

You might get snagged in the habit of playing video games nonstop every day. There is a reason for this—you might be addicted to playing video games! Yes, video game addiction is a real problem! It's even called Internet Video Gaming Disorder. A Common

Sense Media study released in March 2022 found that teens spent an average of gaming in 2021, on either a computer, mobile device, or console. Boys make up the large majority of gamers, with an average of 2 hours and 19 minutes of video gaming daily."[34]

Obviously, if you are playing video games, your arms and legs aren't getting much exercise. This is a very real problem for today's youth. Yes, that's YOU.

The American Psychological Association, the APA, lists these as warning signs of video game addiction. If a young person experiences at least five of these symptoms over a 12-month period, they might have an Internet Gaming Disorder. Can you check the circles?[35]

- Preoccupation with gaming—meaning wanting to game nonstop. Nothing else seems important. Homework and studying certainly are ignored.
- Getting angry or anxious if they cannot play their video games.
- A great need to play more and more games.
- Not interested in other activities like sports or friendships.

- Fabricating and deceiving parents with how long they really are playing.
- Not participating in special classes which help with filling in educational gaps, or after-school programs, or tutoring.
- Escaping into the video world to avoid other emotions to do with coping with negative aspects of life.
- Always want to play longer, no matter if they try to cut it short.
- Never limiting the time they play.

Did you fill all five of these circles? If so, this may be the reason you're having gaps in your education. Perhaps you aren't paying attention to your classes, your lessons, and your homework. Find a way to cut back on your video game time before it's too late!

It's time to buckle down and focus on your health. *Is it healthy for your body and mind to play video games for hours? What could you do instead?*

Helmet & Knee Pad Time

Set your timer for ten minutes.

What you will need for this task:

- Lined notebook
- Pen/Pencil

Think about what changes you could make that might help you avoid video game addiction. If you already think you have a video game addiction, speak with your parents or caregiver. Perhaps they can get you back on track, or they can find someone who can help you.

Write down one change you could make to help you avoid Video Game Addiction.

Chapter Ten

Clean Up on Aisle Ten

As you read this book, hopefully, you have been awakened to the idea that having a dream or a vision of your successful future is important. Having a dream or vision for your future is probably one of the most important achievements of your childhood.

Granted, if you live in an unhealthy emotional home, or live in poverty, or live in gang-infested areas, you might be tempted to say, "This isn't possible for me. I cannot achieve a dream or bring my vision into my future." Others have gone before you and have succeeded. Thousands of children have survived unhealthy emotional homes, they have risen above their poverty by providing their own light and guidance, and by prodding themselves to do their homework and study when there was no one else applauding their success. Thousands of children have kept the vision of their future in their minds as they did their homework, and as they blocked out anything and everything which tried to stand in their way. *Was it easy for these children when they were growing up?* Absolutely not.

Storytime: There was a boy who lived in a chaotic, crazy household full of anger, fighting, alcohol, and drug use by the adults in his home. He wanted to play sports, but he couldn't. He would go straight home after school to make sure his mother was all right. He worried about her the whole time when he tried to listen in school. He was always getting hurt. He broke his arm twice. Sometimes, he got into fights at school. Sometimes, he didn't go to class.

He was only in third grade, but he knew he wanted to be a scientist. It was really difficult to do his homework at home. He could hardly concentrate because the people in his family were always arguing and yelling. He didn't even get a good breakfast, lunch, or dinner. He started making his own lunch so he would not be hungry at school, but sometimes, there was no food in the house to make a lunch for himself.

His mother died when he was fourteen. He started doing bad things and ended up in juvenile detention, but in the back of his mind, he still had his vision. He wanted to be a scientist.

He began to read books. He read lots and lots of books while he was in detention. When he became an adult, he became one of the very important scientists at a very important laboratory in Washington. He knew everything about nuclear energy. He never gave up on his dream. It wasn't easy for him. He was often alone. But he had a vision—a dream—and he worked and worked until he achieved his dream. He got a scholarship to college. He got good grades. He didn't let anything come between him and his dream, though his bad behavior at school had almost ended his dream. He eventually understood that he was the coach of his own life, so he stopped ruining it for himself.

US President Theodore Roosevelt once said, "Nothing in the world is worth having or worth doing unless it means effort, pain, difficulty . . . I have never in my life envied a human being who led an easy life. I have envied a great many people who led difficult lives and led them well".[36]

As the coach of your own life, it's your job and duty to live your life well. You have learned that you are always ultimately in control of you. You make the ultimate decisions for yourself. There isn't always an adult standing next to you telling you "no" or "yes". You have learned that it's of the utmost importance to be a good coach for yourself, and to like or even love yourself, and to make good decisions that help you map out a strong, happy future for yourself.

But—what if you have also realized that you have been on the wrong path?

What if you have already reached a point where you don't care about your grades, or your classes? What if you have already been acting out at school and had a few detentions?

Now What?

Relax. It's not too late for 'clean up on aisle ten." Sometimes, you hear these words over the loudspeaker at a store when a customer accidently breaks a jar or bottle. Someone comes running over with a mop, and before anyone slips in the puddle or gets hurt on the broken glass, it's all cleaned up.

You can do the same for your life. You can 'clean up' what messes might have been made. You CAN get yourself back on track. *Where do you start?*

1. Admit to others you were wrong if you have been acting out in class, at school, or at home. Yep. Own up to any mistakes you have made. You can talk face-to-face, or you can write a note of apology. *Will it make you uncomfortable to have to do this?* Of course, it will, but this is part of re-building your good character, and re-enforcing your strength. Depending on how bad your mistakes were, this might mean quite a few face-to-face apologies or letters.

2. Talk to your parents, your caregivers, your teacher, or your counselor. Explain to them that you know you have some gaps in your education, and explain how you want remedial classes, and help before your gaps become Grand Canyon gaps! Explain how you know that your grades are suffering because of these gaps. Tell these adults to work with you to fill in the gaps and help YOU build a better foundation in your education.

   Teachers, counselors, and principals in

schools are job-bound to get you the help you need to fill in these gaps. If you know, tell them *how* your own brain works and how it learns. Tell them you want to be taught in the mode you learn best. Speak up! You can tell them, "I am the coach of my own life, and I cannot succeed if you don't help me fill in these gaps."

Explain to them that you cannot "do" division because you haven't learned your multiplication tables. Explain that you have tried to learn your multiplication tables, but they never got put into your *long-term memory.* When you explain yourself, like the excellent coach you have become, people WILL listen. Tell them where your gaps are.

3. Do your part. This means studying with a tutor or taking the time to get help on the Internet. It means putting in the effort, or *getting your nails dirty,* to learn what needs to be learned to fill in your identified education gaps.

4. Take the time to develop a dream or a vision. Investigate that dream. Know some of the steps you must take to reach your dream.

Know what type of classes you will need to take to reach your vision. It's NOT too early to begin to have your dream and develop your vision.

Super-Charged-Life

It will be important that adults don't see you as arrogant when you approach them with all your knowledge. You know you can have a super-charged-life when you take the necessary steps to make sure you have learned all you can about your dream or your vision.

A coach has to know how to *play the game.* This means you cannot be the coach of your own life until you know all the rules. This book has tried to make you more aware of how important it is to grab hold of the responsibility of coaching yourself toward your best life possible. You can coach yourself to reach your dreams and your vision.

This is NOT possible if you don't identify your dreams and your vision.

Make the necessary effort to identify your vision for your future as soon as possible.

Do you want to be a musician? Well, start practicing that horn or those drums! *Do you want to be a nurse?* Then, start studying those formulas in science! *Do you want to be a mechanic?* Get help in math if you don't 'get' the metric system.

Some classes might be boring, but they are needed.

Some classes might be difficult, but you can get the help you need to understand what is being taught.

Some of your peers might try to stand in your way, make fun of you, or not support you, but this is the time when you most need to support yourself and help yourself succeed!

Helmet & Knee Pad Time

Set your timer for ten minutes.

What you will need for this task:

- Lined notebook
- Pen/Pencil

This is your last Helmet & Knee Pad Time. It's not important that you do all the suggestions right this moment, but that you eventually DO them.

Ticket to All Games—No Limit to Your Choices!

Write in your notebook, as needed.

- Investigate your future possibilities based on what you like and enjoy doing.
- Decide on a Vision for your future. This isn't your final vision, but a place for you to start.
- State all your goals for your future. Start out with just one or two if it's easier but add to your goals when you want to.
- Write out your objectives to reach your goals. Every goal you have written down for your future needs to have objectives, or steps, to reach your goals. Remember, objectives are the steppingstones to reaching your goal.
- A good coach cheers the team on to success. Cheer for yourself. Tell yourself when you are doing a good job. Don't wait for others to praise you because praise may never come. Cheer yourself on to victory! You deserve a happy life.
- Reward yourself when you achieve an

objective or reach a goal. You can even decide ahead of time what the reward might be.

- Develop friendships with boys who share your values and have their own dreams. Encourage them, as they encourage you.

- Develop mutual support and respect with the boys who share your values.

- Don't let your setbacks discourage you. Each setback is just a learning experience. Keep moving forward, with your eyes on your dream and your vision.

You now know that your dreams can come true—it's all up to you, Coach!

Thank You

Thank you for taking the time to read this book!

If you enjoyed it and found it useful, please take a few minutes to leave a review. It would be appreciated by the author as well as by other teenage boys like you, who want to become the coach of their own life.

Scan this code to leave a review.

About the Author

Ariana Smith is a financial expert, entrepreneur, and writer. Her many years of professional and personal experience through motherhood have nurtured in her a passion for telling inspiring stories to children, teens, and young adults.

She is passionate about empowering young readers to embrace their own identities. Ariana believes in instilling timeless values through history and literature; her mission is to help young generations find their purpose and develop self-confidence and skills that will help them lead fulfilling lives doing what they love.

Ariana's books are written in simple and engaging language and can be read independently by children, teens, or their parents. Her work has proved especially valuable to young readers seeking to develop critical thinking skills.

Ariana loves reading, cooking, and spending time with her beloved husband and their three beautiful children.

Visit Ariana's website to learn more. Sign-up to her newsletter to stay connected and get her upcoming books for free!

www.ariana-smith.com

Read More

An inspiring guide for teenage girls including tips and exercises that will prepare them for the future.

1. Brown, Shelby. "13 (Secretly) Educational Video Games that Kids Will Actually Like".
2. Frontier Communications Parent, Inc.
3. Brown. Ibid.
4. Zippia. "Careers & Jobs". September 9, 2022.
5. Ibid.
6. Dalton, Kyle. "Top 10 Most Popular Athletes". November 2. 2020. Sports Casting.
7. Science News. Stellenbosch University. October 3, 2022.
8. Ibid.
9. Bacharach, Yael. "5 Essential Skills for Successful Coaching". INC. August 8, 2013.
10. Ability Path. "Learning Styles". 2022. Retrieved Google January 1, 2023.
11. Chandler, Warner Gertrude. "Boxcar Children" 1942. Albert Whitman and Co. ©2022.
12. Ferguson, Sian. Gepp, Karin., PsyD. June 22, 2022. "All About Human Personality".
13. Ibid.
14. Firestone, Lisa PhD. "Why We Don't See Ourselves Clearly". PsycAlive© 2022.
15. Davis, Sammy Jr. "I've Gotta Be Me". 1968 Vinyl. Reprise Records.
16. Ibid.
17. Rowe, Mike. "Dirty Jobs" © July 19, 2005.

18. Deering, Sophie. "The Ten Weirdest Jobs in the World". Undercover Recruiter.
19. International Olympic Committee. "Qualities of a Coach" PDF.
20. Ibid.
21. Michael, Jackson. "A Brief History of Goal Posts". September 28, 2015.
22. Shuck, Barry. "Genealogy of American Football: Evolution of Goal Posts. Part One."
23. Matava, Matthew, MD. "Football Injuries in Young Athletes". March, 2019. Ortho-Pinion.
24. Ibid.
25. Ibid.
26. Clark, Diana. "Study Shows Very Masculine Men Are More Likely To Be Happy and Married". Evie. March 24, 2022.
27. Flatly, Margaret. Getty/Seventeen. "32 Cool Outfits for Guys that Instantly Make Them a Million Times Hotter". April 22, 2020.
28. Daniels, Eb. "How to Wear Ascots and Cravats (And What's the Difference?)". Gentleman's Gazette ©2010-2023.
29. Presbyterian Day School. Memphis, TN. Retrieved Google January 7, 2023.
30. Wikipedia. "Transatlantic Tunnel". Retrieved Google January 9, 2023.

31. Lichtcsien, Keith M. “Helping Young People Create Vision”. July, 2011. Resource Strategies.
32. Ibid.
33. Greenlight ©2022 Greenlight Financial Technology, Inc. Patents Pending. The Greenlight card by Community Federal Savings Bank.
34. Newport Academy. “The Latest Research on Teenage Video Game Addiction.” January 6, 2021.
35. Ibid.
36. Goodreads. “Theodore Roosevelt” quotes.

References

Ability Path. “Learning Styles” 2022. abilitypath.org/ap-resources/childrens-learning-styles/

Bacharach, Yael. “5 Essential Skills for Successful Coaching”. INC. August 8, 2013. inc.com/yael-bacharach/five-essential-skills-for-successful-coaching.html

Brown, Shelby. “13 (Secretly) Educational Video Games that Kids Will Actually Like”. October 31, 2022. cnet.com/tech/gaming/13-secretly-educational-video-games-that-kids-will-actually-like/

Chandler, Warner Gertrude. “Boxcar Children” 1942. Albert Whitman and Co. ©2022.

goodreads.com/book/show/297249.The_*Boxcar*Children

Clark, Diana. "Study Shows Very Masculine Men Are More Likely to Be Happy and Married". Evie. March 24, 2022.
eviemagazine.com/post/study-shows-very-masculine-men-are-more-likely-to-be-happy-and-married

Dalton, Kyle. "Top 10 Most Popular Athletes". November 2. 2020. Sports Casting.
sportscasting.com/the-top-10-list-of-most-popular-athletes-in-the-u-s-includes-some-surprising-names/

Daniels, Eb. "How to Wear Ascots and Cravats (And What's the Difference?)". Gentleman's Gazette ©2010-2023.
gentlemansgazette.com/how-to-wear-ascots-cravats/

Davis, Sammy Jr. "I've Gotta Be Me". 1968 Vinyl. Reprise Records.
youtu.be/oaalq3RYAyw

Deering, Sophie. "The Ten Weirdest Jobs in the World". Undercover Recruiter.
theundercoverrecruiter.com/weirdest-jobs-world/

DeLoreto, Caroline. "Psychology For Everyday Life" ©PshcAlive 2022.
psychalive.org/why-we-dont-see-ourselves-clearly/

Fergusson, Sian. Gepp, Karin, PsyD. June 22, 2022. "All About Human Personality".
psychcentral.com/health/what-is-personality

Firestone, Lisa PhD. "Why We Don't See Ourselves Clearly". ©PsycAlive 2022.
psychalive.org/why-we-dont-see-ourselves-clearly/

Flatly, Margaret. Getty/Seventeen. "32 Cool Outfits for Guys that Instantly Make Them a Million Times Hotter". April 22, 2020.
seventeen.com/love/a34297/things-guys-wear-that-make-them-hotter/

Frontier Communications Parent, Inc. © 2022.
frontier.com/resources/e-is-for-everyone-video-game-study

Goodreads. "Theodore Roosevelt" quotes.
goodreads.com/quotes/312751-nothing-in-the-world-is-worth-having-or-worth-doing

Greenlight ©2022 Greenlight Financial Technology, Inc. Patents Pending. The Greenlight card by Community Federal Savings Bank.
greenlight.com/chores-and-allowance-app-for-kids

International Olympic Committee. "Qualities of a Coach" PDF.
stillmed.olympic.org/media/Document%20Library/OlympicOrg/IOC/What-We-Do/Protecting-Clean-Athletes/Athletes-Space/Athletes-Entourage/Coaches/EN-Qualities-of-a-coach.pdf

Kocher, Sarah. US News. New York Office. SWNS Media Group. September 6, 2021.
swnsdigital.com/us/2019/12/these-are-the-most-popular-jobs-kids-dream-of-doing-when-they-grow-up

Lichtcsien, Keith M. "Helping Young People Create Vision". July, 2011. Resource Strategies.
resourcestrategies.com/getattachment/Estate-Planning/Helping-Young-People-Create-Vision-KS.pdf

Matava, Matthew, MD. "Football Injuries in Young Athletes". March, 2019. Ortho-Pinion.
orthoinfo.aaos.org/en/staying-healthy/ortho-pinion-football-injuries-in-young-athletes/

Michael, Jackson. "A Brief History of Goal Posts". September 28, 2015.
thegamebeforethemoney.com/goalposts/

Miller, Mick. "A True Bird's Eye View: Hot Air Balloon Experience". YouTube October 22, 2015. youtu.be/fpvg-7w3PHI

Newport Academy. "The Latest Research on Teenage Video Game Addiction." January 6, 2021. newportacademy.com/resources/treatment/teenage-video-game-addiction/

Osmo. "Exercise Charts for Kids". playosmo.com/kids-learning/exercise-chart-for-kids

Presbyterian Day School. Memphis, TN. pdsmemphis.org/why-pds/building-boys-making-men

Prodigy. "10 Educational Examples to Keep Kids Motivated". April 21, 2022. www.prodigygame.com/main-en/blog/educational-goals/

Rowe, Mike. "Dirty Jobs"© July 19, 2005. MRW Productions; Pilgrim Films & Television; School of Humans.

Science News. Stellenbosch University. October 3, 2022. sciencedaily.com/releases/2022/10/221003132750.htm

Shuck, Barry. "Genealogy of American Football: Evolution of Goal Posts. Part One."June 14, 2022. dawgsbynature.com/2022/6/14/23147890/geneology-of-american-football-evolution-of-goal-posts-part-1

StudyWorkGrow. January 12, 2021. studyworkgrow.com.au/2021/01/12/13-more-unusual-jobs-you-might-not-know-exist/

Wikipedia. "Transaltlantic Tunnel". wikipedia.org/wiki/Transatlantic_tunnel

Youtube. Mister Test. May 6, 2021. "What Kind of Teen are You?"
youtube.com/watch?v=pAsJPy5NOX8

Zippia. "Careers & Jobs". September 9, 2022. zippia.com/professional-athlete-jobs/

Printed in Great Britain
by Amazon